Flower Fairies of the Wayside

POEMS AND PICTURES BY

CICELY MARY BARKER

BLACKIE: LONDON AND GLASGOW

OPEN YOUR EYES!

To shop, and school, to work and play,
The busy people pass all day;
They hurry, hurry, to and fro,
And hardly notice as they go
The wayside flowers, known so well,
Whose names so few of them can tell.

They never think of fairy-folk
Who may be hiding for a joke!

O, if these people understood
What's to be found by field and wood;
What fairy secrets are made plain
By any footpath, road, or lane—
They'd go with open eyes, and *look*
(As you will, when you've read this book),
And then at least they'd learn to see
How pretty **common things can be!**

Distributed in the United States by
Two Continents Publishing Group Ltd.,
30 East 42nd Street, New York, NY 10017

copyright
All rights reserved

Blackie & Son Ltd., Bishopbriggs, Glasgow
450 Edgware Road, London W2 1EG

Printed in Great Britain by Smith and Ritchie Ltd., Edinburgh.

CONTENTS

JACK-BY-THE-HEDGE

" 'Morning, Sir, and how-d'ye-do?
   'Morning, pretty lady!"
That is Jack saluting you,
   Where the lane is shady.

Don't you know him? Straight and tall—
   Taller than the nettles;
Large and light his leaves; and small
   Are his buds and petals.

Small and white, with petals four,
   See his flowers growing!
If you never knew before,
   There is Jack for knowing!

(Jack-by-the-Hedge is also called Garlic Mustard, and Sauce Alone.)

Jack-by-the-hedge

GREATER CELANDINE

You come with the Spring,
  O swallow on high!
You come with the Spring,
  And so do I.

Your nest, I know,
  Is under the eaves;
While far below
  Are my flowers and leaves.

Yet, to and fro
  As you dart and fly,
You swoop so low
  That you brush me by!

I come with the Spring;
  The wall is my home;
I come with the Spring
  When the swallows come.

(The name " Celandine " comes from the Greek word for
" swallow ", and this celandine used sometimes to be called
" swallow-wort ". It has orange-coloured juice in its stems,
and is no relation to the Lesser Celandine, which is in *Flower
Fairies of the Spring*; but it is a relation of the Horned Poppy,
which you will find further on in this book.)

Greater Celandine

GROUND IVY

In Spring he is found;
He creeps on the ground;
But someone's to blame
For the rest of his name—
For Ivy he's *not*!
Oh dear, what a lot
Of muddles we make!
It's quite a mistake,
And really a pity
Because he's so pretty;
He deserves a nice name—
Yes, *someone's* to blame!

(But he *has* some other names, which we do not hear very often; here are four of them: Robin-run-up-the-dyke, Runnadyke, Run-away-Jack, Creeping Charlie.)

Ground Ivy

RED CAMPION

Here's a cheerful somebody,
    By the woodland's edge;
Campion the many-named,
    Robin-in-the-Hedge.

Coming when the bluebells come,
    When they're gone, he stays,
(Round Robin, Red Robin)
    All the summer days.

Soldiers' Buttons, Robin Flower,
    In the lane or wood;
Robin Redbreast, Red Jack,
    Yes, and Robin Hood!

Red Campion

GOOSE-GRASS

Who cares about Goose-Grass? The geese
    do, for sure!
To most other people, I'm common and poor.
By hedges and ditches and dustiest ways
I straggle and climb through my vagabond
    days.
My white little flowers, so few and so wee,
Are almost too few and too tiny to see;
But the children have fun when they find how
    I stick,
And I'm ready to help them play many a
    trick—
So I'm also called " Cleavers "; how firmly
    I cleave,
Wherever I touch you, you'd hardly believe!
    Annoying, maybe,
      But clever of me—
        Yes, clever,
         Oh, clever,
           Most clever of me!

Goose-grass

SCENTLESS MAYWEED

Like a daisy—*not* a daisy!
  (For these leaves of mine
  Aren't a bit like any daisy's—
  They are cut so fine!)

By the cornfield, by the 'lotments,
  By the trodden ways,
Any place will do for Mayweed
  With her snowy rays.

Scentless Mayweed

ROSE-BAY WILLOW-HERB

On the breeze my fluff is blown;
So my airy seeds are sown.

Where the earth is burnt and sad,
I will come to make it glad.

All forlorn and ruined places,
All neglected empty spaces,

I can cover—only think!—
With a mass of rosy pink.

Burst then, seed-pods; breezes, blow!
Far and wide my seeds shall go!

(Another name for this Willow-Herb is " Fireweed ",
because of its way of growing where there have been heath
or forest fires.)

Rose-bay Willow-herb

BLACK MEDICK

" Why are we called 'Black', sister,
　When we've yellow flowers?"
" I will show you why, brother:
　See these seeds of ours?
Very soon each tiny seed
　Will be turning black indeed!"

Black Medick

BEE ORCHIS

In the grass o' the bank, by the side o' the
    way,
        Where your feet may stray
        On your luckiest day,
There's a sight most rare that your eyes may
    see:
  A beautiful orchis that looks like a bee!
  A velvety bee, with a proud little elf,
  Who looks like the wonderful orchis him-
    self—
        In the grass o' the hill,
        Not often, but still
        Just once in a way
        On your luckiest day!

Bee Orchis

WHITE BINDWEED

O long long stems that twine!
O buds, so neatly furled!
O great white bells of mine
(None purer in the world),
Each lasting but one day!
O leafy garlands, hung
In wreaths beside the way—
Well may your praise be sung!

(But this Bindweed, which is a big sister to the little pink
Field Convolvulus, is not good to have in gardens, though it is
so beautiful; because it winds around other plants and trees.
One of its names is " Hedge Strangler ". Morning Glories are
a garden kind of Convolvulus.)

White Bindweed

RED CLOVER

The Fairy: O, what a great big bee
Has come to visit me!
He's come to find my honey.
O, what a great big bee!

The Bee: O, what a great big Clover!
I'll search it well, all over,
And gather all its honey.
O, what a great big Clover!

Red Clover

SELF-HEAL

When little elves have cut themselves,
    Or Mouse has hurt her tail,
Or Froggie's arm has come to harm,
    This herb will never fail.
The Fairy's skill can cure each ill
    And soothe the sorest pain;
She'll bathe, and bind, and soon they'll find
    That they are well again.

(This plant was a famous herb of healing in old days, as you can tell by the names it was given—Self-Heal, All-Heal, and others. It is also called Prunella.)

Self-heal

RUSH-GRASS
AND COTTON-GRASS

Safe across the moorland
   Travellers may go,
If they heed our warning—
   We're the ones who know!

Let the footpath guide you—
   You'll be safely led;
There is bog beside you
   Where you cannot tread!

Mind where you are going!
   If you turn aside
Where you see us growing,
   Trouble will betide.

Keep you to the path, then!
   Hark to what we say!
Else, into the quagmire
   You will surely stray.

Rush-grass and Cotton-grass

STORK'S-BILL

" Good morning, Mr. Grasshopper!
   Please stay and talk a bit!"
" Why yes, you pretty Fairy;
   Upon this grass I'll sit.
And let us ask some riddles;
   They're better fun than chat:
Why am I like the Stork's-bill?
   Come, can you answer *that?*"

" Oh no, you clever Grasshopper!
   I fear I am a dunce;
I cannot guess the answer—
   I give it up at once!"
" When children think they've caught me,
   I'm gone, with leap and hop;
And when they gather Stork's-bill,
   Why, all the petals drop!"

(The Stork's-bill gets her name from the long seed-pod, which looks like a stork's beak or bill. Others of the family are called Crane's-bills.)

Stork's-bill

SOW THISTLE

I have handsome leaves, and my stalk is tall,
  And my flowers are prettily yellow;
Yet nobody thinks me nice at all:
  They think me a tiresome fellow—
    An ugly weed
    And a rogue indeed;
  For wherever I happen to spy,
    As I look around,
    That they've dug their ground,
  I say to my seeds " Go, fly!"

And because I am found
On the nice soft ground,
A trespassing weed am I!

(But I have heard that Sow Thistle is good rabbit-food, so
perhaps it is not so useless as most people think.)

Sow Thistle

TOTTER-GRASS

The leaves on the tree-tops
   Dance in the breeze;
Totter-grass dances
   And sways like the trees—

Shaking and quaking!
   While through it there goes,
Dancing, a Fairy,
   On lightest of toes.

(Totter-grass is also called Quaking-grass.)

Totter-grass

TANSY

In busy kitchens, in olden days,
Tansy was used in a score of ways;
Chopped and pounded, when cooks would
  make
Tansy puddings and tansy cake,
Tansy posset, or tansy tea;
Physic or flavouring tansy'd be.
          People who know
          Have told me so!

That is my tale of the past; today,
Still I'm here by the King's Highway,
Where the air from the fields is fresh and
  sweet,
With my fine-cut leaves and my flowers neat.
Were ever such button-like flowers seen—
Yellow, for elfin coats of green?
          Three in a row—
          I stitch them so!

Tansy

RIBWORT PLANTAIN

Hullo, Snailey-O!
How's the world with *you*?
Put your little horns out;
Tell me how you do?
There's rain, and dust, and sunshine,
Where carts go creaking by;
You like it wet, Snailey;
I like it dry!

Hey ho, Snailey-O,
I'll whistle you a tune!
I'm merry in September
As e'er I am in June.
By any stony roadside
Wherever you may roam,
All the summer through, Snailey,
Plantain's at home!

(There are some other kinds of Plantain besides this. The
one with wide leaves, and tall spikes of seed which canaries
enjoy, is Greater Plantain.)

Ribwort Plantain

FUMITORY

Given me hundreds of years ago,
My name has a meaning you shall know:
It means, in the speech of the bygone folk,
" Smoke of the Earth "—a soft green smoke!

A wonderful plant to them I seemed;
Strange indeed were the dreams they dreamed,
Partly fancy and partly true,
About " Fumiter " and the way it grew.

Where men have ploughed or have dug the
    ground,
Still, with my rosy flowers, I'm found;
Known and prized by the bygone folk
As " Smoke of the Earth "—a soft green
    smoke!

(The name " Fumitory " was " Fumiter " 300 years ago;
and long before that, " Fume Terre ", which is the French
name, still, for the plant. " Fume " means " smoke ", " terre "
means " earth ".)

Fumitory

HORNED POPPY

These are the things I love and know:
The sound of the waves, the sight of the sea;
The great wide shore when the tide is low;
Where there's salt in the air, it's home to me—
With my petals of gold—the home for me!

The waves come up and cover the sand,
Then turn at the pebbly slope of the beach;
I feel the spray of them, where I stand,
Safe and happy, beyond their reach—
With my marvellous horns—beyond their
reach!

Horned Poppy

CHICORY

By the white cart-road,
　Dusty and dry,
Look! there is Chicory,
　Blue as the sky!

Or, where the footpath
　Goes through the corn,
See her bright flowers,
　Each one new-born!

Though they fade quickly,
　O, have no sorrow!
There will be others
　New-born to-morrow!

(Chicory is also called Succory.)

Chicory

JACK-GO-TO-BED-AT-NOON

I'll be asleep by noon!
Though bedtime comes so soon,
    I'm busy too.
Twelve puffs!—and then from sight
I shut my flowers tight;
Only by morning light
    They're seen by you.

Then, on some day of sun,
They'll open wide, each one,
    As something new!
Shepherd, who minds his flock,
Calls it a Shepherd's Clock,
Though it can't say " tick-tock "
    As others do!

(Another of Jack's names, besides Shepherd's Clock, is
Goats' Beard.)

Jack-go-to-bed-at-noon

CAT'S EAR

I am not Dandelion's self,
   But Dandelion's kin;
His stem is full of milky juice,
   But mine is tough and thin.

My leaves, as soft as pussies' ears,
   Are clustered on the ground;
To make the dry waste places gay
   My yellow flowers abound.

(Cat's Ear is one of many flowers, all a little different from
each other, that are something like Dandelions.)

Cat's Ear

AGRIMONY

Spikes of yellow flowers,
   All along the lane;
When the petals vanish,
   Burrs of red remain.

First the spike of flowers,
   Then the spike of burrs;
Carry them like soldiers,
   Smartly, little sirs!

Agrimony

AUTHOR'S NOTE

I believe that many children would be glad to know how much of this book, and of the others in the Flower Fairy series, is true, and how much " pretend ". So, let me say quite plainly, that I have drawn all the plants and flowers very carefully, from real ones; and everything that I have said about them is as true as I could make it. But I have never seen a fairy; the fairies and all about them are just " pretend ". (It is nice to pretend about fairies.) Now, I think, children will be able to tell the true parts from the pretend parts in these books.

I have gleaned from many sources my information about the flowers, their country names, and so on; but am especially indebted to the beautiful series of books *Wild Flowers as they Grow*, by G. Clarke Nuttall (Cassell); and am grateful also for the help I have been given at Kew Gardens.

C. M. B.